Fun Dog Facts for
Kids 9 - 12

Fun Animal Facts fo 1

Jacquelyn Eln. ohnson

Crimson Hill
Books

www.CrimsonHillBooks.com/best-pets-for-kids

First edition, October 2016.

Cataloguing in Publication Data

Pulsifer, Tristan | Johnson, Jacquelyn Elnor

Fun Dog Facts for Kids 9-12

Description: Crimson Hill Books trade paperback edition | Nova Scotia, Canada

ISBN 978-1-988650-36-4 (Paperback)

BISAC: JNF003060 Juvenile Nonfiction: Animals - Dogs |JNF003170 Juvenile Nonfiction: Animals - Pets JNF051150 Juvenile Nonfiction: Science & Nature - Zoology

THEMA: WNGD - Dogs as pets | YNNH1 - Children's / Teenage general interest: Pets & pet care: dogs | YNNJ21 - Children's / Teenage general interest: Dogs & wolves

Record available at https://www.bac-lac.gc.ca/eng/Pages/home.aspx

Book design: Jesse Johnson

Crimson Hill Books
(a division of)
Crimson Hill Products Inc.
Wolfville, Nova Scotia
Canada

A happy boy and and his dog playing in a pool. Photo courtesy of OceangreenSA on Pixabay.

This is Pip. He's a Bouvier puppy.

Why do dogs live with people?

Have you ever asked why dogs would want to live with people?

And why do people want to live with dogs?

Why don't we live with goats, or sheep, or even foxes instead of puppies and dogs?

Why did dogs choose people? Why did people choose dogs?

No one can be sure of the answers. We don't know exactly when dogs and people decided they like each other and want to live together. Scientists say it was probably at least 15,000 years ago. But it could have been longer.

Dogs joining people happened before people learned how to write. We can't read their stories about what happened. So, we really don't know very much about how ancient people lived.

We do know that dogs and people got together before people learned to live in one place.

At that time, people lived in small family groups. They were nomads. This means they followed the herds of the animals they hunted, always moving in search of food.

They didn't have permanent homes. They were always travelling, stopping only a short time to camp before moving on.

Wild dogs would have followed these people. Dogs noticed that there were food scraps and bones the people threw away. For a very long time, dogs were still wild, but they liked to live near where people hunted, made fires and ate meat. There were tasty bones for the dogs.

At some point, people took some of the puppies, tamed them and taught them how to help people hunt or fish. Other dogs might have pulled sleds or helped carry things when the people moved to a new place.

Dogs were also useful to watch over the people as they slept. Dogs protected people from wild animals like bears and wolves.

People found it easy to care for dogs, who mostly looked after themselves. All dogs wanted was the same as what the people wanted for themselves. This was clean water to drink, food to eat and warm places near the fire to sleep.

People found that dogs could be useful. Dogs helped with hunting, carrying things, protecting campsites and even helped keep people warm on winter nights. Dogs could be cute and funny, too.

People came to respect dogs for the work they did. They enjoyed having them around.

Dogs decided they liked people. They learned how to communicate with people to get food, water and shelter. Some people and some dogs became good friends. They helped each other, as friends do.

This probably happened many thousands of years before cats became pets. This was also long before people used any other animal to do work for them.

Dogs were the first animal to get to know people.

Today, we call dogs, "man's best friend." This means they are the animal that is the best friend to people. Dogs are close to humans in the ways our bodies work, the ways we think and behave and how we live. One of the reasons we like dogs is they are a lot like us.

Dogs need lots of exercise to stay healthy. They need at least two walks or runs every day.

Dogs have changed a lot to be able to live with people. But it is also true that having dogs has changed how people live. Mostly, dogs and people have made each others' lives better.

Can you think of more ways dogs help people? If you have a pet dog, how do they help you?

Do dogs see better than people?

Most dogs have only average vision. If they were people, they'd probably need glasses or contact lenses.

But dogs can see better than us when there isn't very much light. That's on cloudy days or early in the morning and just before dark. Like us, dogs can't see at all when it is completely dark.

Dogs have better peripheral vision than people have. Peripheral (say this word like this: purr-if-fur-ral) means side vision. Dogs can see both what's in front of them and what's beside them much better than we can.

Do dogs see in colour? Yes and no. To a dog, everything is blue, green, yellowish-green or gray. They can't see red the way most humans can. To them, red looks the same as gray or black.

Something people can't do but many animals can is see in ultraviolet (UV) light. Creatures that can see UV light are reindeer, hedgehogs, some reptiles, bees, birds, some fish, cats and dogs.

Since people can't see UV light, we can't say for certain what it looks like. We think it's probably like what people can see when they wear night vision goggles.

When there is hardly any light, wearing night vision goggles makes everything different shades of gray. It looks like a black-and-white photograph.

This is a Labrador Retriever puppy. Labs are the most popular pet dog in the United States and Canada.

So the answer to this question is dogs see better than people in some ways and about the same as people in other ways.

Do dogs have jobs?

Until not very long ago, almost every dog that wasn't wild had a job.

Dogs did many different jobs for people. They could herd farm animals like sheep and goats. They could be companion animals to horses and other farm animals. Dogs could also protect farm animals and their owners from predators. Predators means animals that want to attack people and their animals.

Dalmatians became known as fire station dogs. They were trained to clear the path for the horses pulling firewagons. Before there were firetrucks, water for putting out fires was loaded into tanks. These tanks were on firewagons. Horses pulled these wagons to where the fire was. The fire station horses were guided through the crowds of people on city streets by the fire station dogs.

Dalmatians are big enough to do this work and they're good at it. They helped guide the fire station horses to the fire. They also helped keep the fire horses calm in all the noise and confusion of a fire.

Today, water is pumped by the trucks using hoses attached to fire hydrants. We no longer need Dalmatians to make way for the trucks, because modern fire trucks have sirens.

Today, most Dalmatians are pets.

Modern dogs can do many jobs.

Dogs work as actors in videos, plays, movies and TV shows.

They're guard dogs for businesses and homeowners.

Another job some dogs have is playing with and entertaining children. Or serving as cheerful visitors to very elderly and sick people in care homes. Or being a helper service dog to people who are ill or who have disabilities.

Dogs have been companions to people for many thousands of years, both at work and at home.

Dogs are smart and eager to please people. This makes it possible to train them to do many specialized jobs.

Some dogs have very unusual and important jobs. These are jobs people can't do nearly as well or at all.

Have you ever been at the airport and seen an officer with a dog that was leaping onto the baggage carousels and sniffing everyone's luggage? This working dog was looking for things people might have put in their suitcases that they are not allowed to travel with. Some of these things you can't travel with are some types of food and illegal drugs.

Smelling these things when they're packed away is something humans can't do. But dogs, with their super-sniffer noses, can.

Police and military officers also use sniffer dogs to find other dangerous things, such as bombs.

Search-and-rescue teams use dogs to save people who are drowning, lost or buried after a mountain avalanche or an earthquake.

This is a Beagle Puppy.

Assistance dogs help people who are blind or cannot hear, acting as their eyes and ears and helping them have better lives.

Specially-trained companion dogs can help people who must rely on their wheelchair to fetch things, turn lights on and off and help open and close doors.

Other types of companion dogs help people with serious illnesses be healthier and happier.

There might be someone at your school or youth group who has a companion dog. If so, you could ask them how their dog helps them.

When you see a working dog, remember he or she is at work if they have their harness on. Don't go near them or touch them without permission from their owner. If they have their harness off, the dog knows it is playtime and might want to say "Hello" to you.

This is the poster for Rinty's first starring role in Where the North Begins in 1923. By Warner Bros-Lithograph by Otis Lithograph, Cleveland (site poster) [Public domain], via Wikimedia Commons.

The Amazing Story of Rin-tin-tin

Some dogs appear in movies, TV shows and advertisements.

The very first dog to become an international movie star was Rin-tin-tin. He was a German Shepherd puppy who was just five days old when a U.S. Army Air Service soldier, Corporal Lee Duncan, rescued him, his litter mates and their mother.

Rinty, his mother and his brothers and sisters were the only dogs still alive at a German training centre for breeding military dogs. The training centre had been destroyed in a 1918 bombing raid. This was during World War I in France.

Corporal Duncan took pity on the tiny, wounded pups and their starving mother and took them back to camp. He gave the mother and most of the pups away to his fellow officers.

Corporal Duncan decided to keep two of the puppies, a male and a female. He named his pups Rin-tin-tin and Nanette. All three of them survived the war. When the war was over, they headed home to Los Angeles in California.

Sadly, Nanette died of pneumonia on the way to Corporal Duncan's home. But Rin-tin-tin was healthy and loved to learn tricks. Mr. Duncan thought that he would show off these tricks and his clever German Shepherd in dog shows.

Then a friend took a movie-camera video of Rinty doing his tricks. When he watched this video, Mr. Duncan got the idea to see if his handsome dog could be in movies. In 1922, Rinty got a small role in a movie. He played a wolf. The director thought he was a good actor.

Then a magical thing happened. People loved seeing Rinty. They wanted more movies with a dog hero. Rinty became a big movie star, almost overnight! In his very next movie, *Where the North Begins*, he got the staring role!

Soon, Rinty and his owner were famous. People everywhere wanted to meet them. Rinty signed all his contracts with Warner Brothers movie studio with his paw print.

Rinty would make 27 movies in his 10-year career. He died in 1932, at age 14. There have been many other dogs (some of them Rinty's grand-pups and great-grand-pups) who played the role of Rin-tin-tin in movies and on TV ever since.

Rinty wasn't the very first dog in movies, but he was the first to become famous around the world and will never be forgotten.

Since his time, there have been other famous dog actors in movies and on TV. Lassie is another movie-star dog who started out as an unwanted puppy.

Timmie (played by actor Jon Provost) and Lassie (Pal) in the Lassie show on television.

Lassie's Story

Pal was a collie puppy who just wouldn't stop barking. He liked to chase motorcycles. He chewed everything. His owners decided to take him to Rudd Weatherwax, a dog trainer, to see if their puppy could learn how to be a better pet.

Mr. Weatherwax trained dogs to be in the movies. This was in 1940, when lots of movies were being made. There were often dog actors in these movies.

But soon, Pal the dog would be the most famous of them all.

Pal was a big dog, as male collies are. He quickly learned to stop peeing in the house, stop chewing everything and not bark so much. But he didn't want to stop chasing motorcycles!

His owners decided he was just too much trouble, so they gave Pal to Mr. Weatherwax. Pal was happy to be a family pet. He soon learned how to go and find the Weatherwax children when it was dinner time.

One day, Mr. Weatherwax took Pal to the MGM movie studio and asked for a screen test. Pal passed this test because he was smart and well-trained as well as being a friendly, handsome dog.

In his very first scene of his very first movie, *Lassie Come Home*, Pal had to wait for a command, then jump out of a boat and swim to shore. He had to come out of the water at exactly where the movie camera operator was waiting. The next shot would be Pal coming up on shore, looking exhausted.

Pal sat patiently in the boat, then leapt into the water when he got the command. He swam to the exact place on shore he'd been told to go to. He walked out of the water looking like a hero.

He'd shown his movie star power from the very first scene he was in. Everyone was delighted with his performance.

Pal would star in six more Lassie movies. Even though in the stories sometimes Lassie is hurt, Pal was always kindly treated. If his paws were bleeding in the story, this was really make-up.

Pal and Mr. Weatherwax were invited everywhere. They went to hospitals to cheer up sick children. They had a radio show. They did other celebrity appearances at department stores and dog shows.

Lassie (Pal) got his own star on the Hollywood Walk of Fame!

Then, television producer Robert Maxwell asked if Mr. Weatherwax and Pal wanted to do a Lassie show on TV. The show started on TV in 1954.

Pal had the honor of choosing his co-star for the Lassie TV shows! He met the three boys who the producers thought would be good actors to play the role of Timmie, Lassie's owner. The people making the show chose the boy that Pal liked the best!

But by now, Pal was getting older. He didn't have the energy of a young dog any more. He couldn't do all the running and jumping the scripts called for. One of his sons, Lassie Junior, did most of the work on the television set. Pal had his own dog bed and watched over everything that happened.

Of course, all the crew and other actors were happy to pet and spoil Pal. He made friends everywhere.

In the Lassie books, Lassie is a female. But the dog actors who portray Lassie are always male. This is because male collies are larger.

Female collies also lose their coat from time to time. This makes them look different. Males don't do this, so when groomed properly they look the same all the

No dog can resist a ballgame! This one is a labradoodle, part labrador retriever, part poodle. Photo courtesy of Pixabay by Spoda

time. (Grooming means having their long hair brushed every day).

Pal, the first Lassie, was 18 years old – very old for a collie – when he died in 1958. From then until 2000, the Weatherwax family bred and trained all the Lassies for television and special appearances. These were always sons, grandsons and great-grandsons of Pal.

Today, a friend of the Weatherwax family carries on this tradition. The current Lassie is a tenth-generation grandson of Pal, the naughty puppy who became a movie star!

A dog's tail. Photo by Stux on Pixabay.

Why do dogs have tails?

A dog uses her tail for balance. It helps her run and jump.

In ancient times, some people believed that if they cut off a dog's tail, the dog would not get a terrible illness dogs can get called rabies. This isn't true. Today, we give dogs their shots so they don't get illnesses like rabies.

A dog that is always turning around in circles and chasing their tail isn't a happy dog. They are probably doing this because they are very bored, not getting enough walks and attention or they are distressed. If your dog is always doing this, you might need help from a dog trainer to learn ways to help your dog be happier.

This will mean that you must work with your dog to help him learn not to do the odd behaviour. You want your dog to do something much better instead, like want to go outside to play with you.

Can dogs eat fruit and vegetables?

Dogs have lived with people for so long that they have learned to eat and enjoy most of the foods that people eat. (There are some exceptions. For example, Dalmatians can't eat meat.)

Most dogs can eat most fruits and vegetables.

Dogs need to eat a quality brand of dog food that is designed especially for your dog's type and age. These deliver the right nutrition to your dog to keep him healthy. The directions on the can or bag tell you how much to feed your dog every day. The bag, box or can of food will also list what is in the food.

Very young puppies and dogs that are sick might need special food. But most dogs eat kibble, or dog chow. It is dry chunks of food.

Your vet can also recommend what to feed your dog and how much.

Sometimes, for a treat, dogs can have a taste of people food. There are some foods we eat that are good for them and some that dogs should never have.

Bananas, cranberries, pears, raspberries and blueberries are all safe for dogs to eat. So are apples, oranges and watermelon.

Vegetables that dogs can have are carrot sticks, green beans, cucumber or zucchini slices and baked potatoes.

Tired puppy. Photo by Chiemsee2016 on Pixabay.

Be careful to never let dogs have apple seeds. Apple seeds have arsenic in them. Arsenic is a poison. Don't let dogs have pits from peaches and plums! These pits have another poison in them called "cyanide." Eating raw potatoes will also make dogs sick.

These are the plant foods (this means nuts, fruits and vegetables) that are especially dangerous for dogs to eat and could make them very ill:

- Chocolate
- Avocados
- Onions or anything in the onion family such as leeks and garlic
- Grapes or raisins
- Macadamia nuts. Just six macadamia nuts can make a dog very seriously ill.

This tiny chihuahua pup fits in a tea cup. Photo courtesy of Pixabay by Teerasuwat.

What is the smallest dog?

The Chihuahua (say it like this: Chi-wah-wah) is the smallest dog breed.

Chihuahuas only get to be between two and six pounds (a little less than 1 kg. to just under 3 kg.) when they are adults.

But it was a Yorkshire Terrier who was the smallest dog ever known. Her name was Pinocchio.

She lived in England and weighed just four ounces (113 grams) when she was an adult.

She was just 2 ½ inches (6.5 cm) tall. That's small enough to fit in a tea cup!

Dogs love to do anything fun, either with you or with other dogs.

What is the biggest dog?

The largest dog ever known was Zorba, an Old English Mastiff who weighed 343 pounds (155.5 kg.). That's about as much as two adult men weigh if they stepped on the scale at the same time!

Zorba was more than 8 feet (2.4 meters) long, from his nose to his tail! That's one huge dog!

This is an adult Saint Bernard.

The tallest dog breed is the Irish Wolfhound, but they are usually a sleek, thin dog. They can grow to be 35 inches (almost a meter) tall!

Another dog breed that is usually very large is the Great Dane.

The dog that usually weighs the most (and eats the most food) is the Saint Bernard.

Can dogs smell the time?

Here is a question that fooled scientists for a very long time. But now we know the answer!

How does your dog know what time you get home from school? Does she sit at the door all day and wait for you to come back? Or does she know how to tell time, so she can be waiting for you just before you walk in the door?

This question was a mystery for a long time. Scientists were stumped. Lots of dog owners knew their pets could tell time. But how can dogs possibly do this, when no other animal can?

No one had a clue. Finally, after doing lots of tests, scientists discovered that dogs can smell time. This is a very new discovery! Here's how dogs do it.

When you and your family are at home, you're leaving little bits of your odour everywhere in the house. Your dog, with her excellent smelling abilities, recognizes your smell. When you're at home, your scent is strong for your pets.

Of all the types of pets there are, dogs are the best at smelling things. They recognize scents and they also notice how much of a certain scent there is in the air.

After you leave the house, your smell begins to get less. It keeps getting less and less as the day goes on. So, your smell might be strong to your dog when you're at home and in the morning, right after you leave for school or errands.

Dogs can get an amazing amount of information with just one sniff!

As the day goes by, that smell gradually decreases. Your dog notices exactly what the smell level is at the time of day that you usually get home.

She has learned that exact amount of your smell means you come in the door. Just before then, she might sit looking out the window, watching for you to appear so she can rush to the door and greet you.

Dogs use their incredible noses to know when it's time for their walks, for other family members to get home and (this is important to know) when it's time for dinner. Their smell-clock tells them everything they need to know about their regular routines.

Just like people, dogs like routines. They like to know what's going to happen and when.

And that's why dogs learned to smell time!

This happy boy is a Golden Retriever.

Why do dogs have extra eyelids?

Dogs have an upper eyelid (like people do), a lower eyelid and a third eyelid, called a "haw." The haw helps keep their eyes moist and protected.

You could look very closely at a dog's (or a cat's) eye and never see their haw. It is hidden in the inner corner of their eye.

An amazing thing their haws can do is brush across their eyes to clean them. It works just like a windshield wiper on a car works to clear off the window shield (windscreen).

Why are there different breeds of dogs?

Extremely long ago, both cats and dogs came from the same ancestor animal. They are very distantly related.

Both modern wolves and dogs came from the same wolf ancestor long ago.

Dogs and wolves are still close enough that if you have a male wolf and a female dog, they could have puppies that are half wolf, half dog.

At first, all dogs that lived with people were the same. But gradually, people began to breed dogs for specific abilities, body size and shape and appearance.

This means people chose the puppies that could do jobs they wanted done or looked a certain way. They wanted dogs that were small, or large or medium-sized.

Ones with short hair, or long hair.

Ones with a long pointy nose, or a small nose.

Ones that could learn to swim and rescue people who were drowning, or pull a sled, or climb a ladder, or just be cute and cuddly.

When these special puppies were adults, they bred them to get more pups just like the parents.

In this way, people invented all the pure breeds of dogs there are today.

Some of these breeds are good at hunting. Some are good at swimming. Some are good at herding sheep or goats. Some just look cute, or funny, or odd.

Today, the breeds of dogs are grouped together, according to what those dogs can do very well, what they look like and their usual behaviour.

These are the modern breeds of dogs according to the American Kennel Club:

1. The **Herding Group** of dogs help farmers look after their animals. They are intelligent and hard workers. Some breeds in this group are Australian Cattle Dogs, Bouviers, Collies, German Shepherds, Sheepdogs and Corgis.

2. The **Hound Group** are hunters. Sighthounds are especially good at seeing big animals like deer, moose and wild boar. Scenthounds are especially good at sniffing out small game animals where they hide, like rabbits. Some dogs in the Hound Group are Beagles, Basset Hounds, Dachshunds and Whippets.

3. The **Non-Sporting Group** includes dogs who once had jobs, but now are mostly pets. Some of these are Dalmatians, Bulldogs and Poodles.

4. The **Sporting Group** help hunters by being pointers, setters and retrievers. They are popular family pets because they are trainable and loyal. Some dogs in this group are Irish Setters, Labrador Retrievers, Golden Retrievers, Spaniels and Vizslas.

This is a Norwich Terrier. They're from the UK.

5. The **Terriers** have their own group. They were originally bred to get rid of rats, foxes, weasels and other 'pest' creatures. Some breeds of terriers are Miniature Schnauzers, Scottish Terriers, Border Terriers and Airedales.

6. **Toy breeds** have strong personalities in a small body! They are Chihuahuas, Pekingese, Pomeranians, Pugs and Japanese Chins.

7. **Working breeds** are large dogs still bred to do certain jobs, such as Great Danes, Boxers, Newfoundlanders and Huskies.

All dogs that aren't these breeds are called mixed-breed dogs. Mixed breeds can be a cross between two recognized breeds. One of these is the Labradoodle, which is half Labrador Retriever and half Standard Poodle (the Standard Poodle is the largest type of Poodle).

Or a mixed-breed dog could be a mix of many types.

How long do dogs live?

The good news is that many pet dogs are living for longer than they used to. The reason is they get better food and better care, including regular health check-ups at the veterinarian's office.

Wild dogs aren't nearly so lucky. They usually live only a few years.

With care, pet dogs usually live about 11 to 13 years.

Smaller dogs often live longer than the larger breeds. For small dogs, living for 15 years isn't unusual.

Occasionally, dogs live even longer than this. A surprising fact is that city dogs usually live longer than country dogs. One reason might be that city dogs are most likely to be walking on a leash and less likely to be hit by a car.

The oldest known dog was Bluey, an Queensland Heeler who lived in Australia. His job was herding sheep. He lived to a very old age for a dog and died when he was 29 years old.

This is a greyhound right before a race.

How fast can a dog run?

Of all the breeds of dogs that have ever been tested, Greyhounds are the best at seeing. They also are the fastest at running. For these reasons, if you go to dog races, the dogs you will see will be greyhounds.

They run races when they are young, and then usually retire to become family pets.

Most dogs can run as fast as about 20 miles per hour (or just a bit faster than 32 kilometers per hour). Greyhounds would leave all these dogs far behind. They can run as fast as 45 miles per hour (or 72.4 kilometers per hour).

That's not nearly fast enough to beat a cheetah. They can run 75 miles per hour (120.7 kilometers per hour).

A cheetah cub with a puppy.

Dogs racing a cheetah would still win if it was a long race. That's because cheetahs can't run that fast for very long. They quickly run out of energy.

All cats can run fast, but only in short bursts. Dogs, like people, are built for long-distance running.

So, if all these animals were running a race against the fastest human runner, who do you think would win?

The fastest human runner alive today is Usain Bolt. His fastest time is 27.8 miles per hour (or 44.72 kilometers per hour). He'd easily beat most dogs. It might be a very close tie with a Greyhound, but the cheetah would likely win the race – or quit long before the finish line because he was exhausted!

This Boxer is panting to cool off.

Do dogs sweat?

Dogs sweat, but not like people do. They only sweat through the pads of their paws.

Most dogs love to swim. One of the benefits for them is they can cool off in the hot weather, the same reason people like to swim.

Dogs also have another way of cooling off. They pant to draw more cooling air into their bodies. Dogs can take 300 to 400 breaths every minute by panting. With normal breathing, they take about 35 breaths a minute.

A close-up photo of a dog's whiskers.

Why do dogs have whiskers?

Do you think your dog would look better if only he didn't have those strange hairs on his face? Are you thinking you should cut them off?

Don't do it! Dogs need their whiskers to help them make sense of the world. Whiskers tell a dog about how big the space he wants to walk through or push his head through actually is.

Whiskers also tell dogs other things, with super abilities that humans don't have. One example is that dogs can sense when storms are coming or there is going to be an earthquake.

Many other animals can also do this. For dogs, it seems that their whiskers are part of their sensing tools (others are nose, ears and eyes) that give them this information.

It's probably true that whiskers do much more for dogs that we don't know about yet. It's one of the fascinating things still to be discovered about dogs!

These are Norwegian Lundehunds.

Why do some dogs have 24 toes?

The Norwegian Lundehund was bred by Vikings as a hunting dog. Today, this dog is quite rare. It's also quite unusual.

All dogs have five toes on each foot, just like humans. But Norwegian Lundehunds have six toes on each foot, or a total of 24 toes. These extra toes don't seem to make much difference to how well Lundehunds walk or run on their extra-large feet. It's just a quirky thing about them.

Dogs and cats can be friends.

Do dogs hate cats?

The idea that all dogs hate cats is a very old one.

It isn't true. Even though dogs and cats are quite different in the ways they think and behave, they can become friends.

This doesn't just happen. Pet owners need to teach their pets to get along and treat each other well.

Introduce your pets to each other gently, being sure than no one feels jealous or left out (or worries that someone else will eat their food).

You know this won't happen, but pets don't. They need patience and loving kindness to build trust in you to always take good care of them.

Every pet deserves to feel comfortable and secure in his or her home.

If you have a dog that chases your cat, this is bad behaviour. It must change.

Here's what to do. When you see your dog making signs that another chase is about to start (he'll be staring at the cat and might be whining or growling) call out your dog's name loudly. When your dog turns to look at you, praise him and give him a treat.

What you are doing is teaching him that there is something much better to do than chase the cat.

Keep doing this and he will learn that you won't allow cat chasing.

Dogs are a lot like little children who are about two years old. Shouting, "No!" when they do something wrong just scares them. They don't understand. What works is to change what they're doing right now by offering them something better to do.

They will keep testing you, just to see what happens when they repeat the bad behaviour. If you keep changing what they're paying attention to in that moment, they soon learn what they aren't allowed to do.

Also, like little children, dogs like to know there are rules and that the rules are always the same. They want to know what will please you. Use this to help all your pets become good friends.

This is a lavender pomeranian.

What colours are dogs' coats?

Dogs have skin covered in hair. Their skin and hair is called a coat.

Their coats can be all one colour or a mix of two or more colours. These colours are the same as the natural hair colours that people have. These are: white, black, brown, tan (a brownish-white), red, orange-brown, yellow-gold and grey.

One breed of dog isn't any of these colours. It's the Lavender Pomeranian. Lavender is an herb with purple flowers. Though that's its name, this dog isn't really purple. It's a blue-black colour that looks purplish.

Lavender Pomeranians are one of the dog breeds that are very rare.

Why do dogs bark?

There is only one breed of dog that can't bark. It is the Basenji, also called the African Wolf Dog.

All other breeds of dogs and mixed breed dogs yip, bark, whine and howl for many different reasons.

Some breeds are more likely to be barkers than others.

They might think they are protecting their yard or home, or they are barking because of a loud noise like the doorbell or phone ringing. They could be barking because they've been left home alone and want attention.

Dogs are pack animals. A pack is a family group. Dogs need to be with others to be happy.

They need to be with their pack so they know what to do. Their pack makes them feel safe.

When dogs bark, it could be they've been inside too long and they need exercise. They could be afraid. Or anxious. Or sounding a warning about something dangerous, like a fire.

If you have a dog that barks a lot and there doesn't seem to be any reason, it could just be she wants more active playtime with you. Getting lots of exercise can solve many 'bad dog' problems.

These Standard Poodle puppies have a puppy cut. Their hair is the same length all over, not like a Poodle cut.

What makes French Poodles French?

French poodles aren't French at all, though they are a popular breed in France and many other places in the world.

Poodles were first bred in Germany to retrieve ducks, geese and other birds that hunters had shot. The birds would fall into lakes or ponds and the poodles would leap in to get them. The Germans called this dog a *pudelhund*, which means splashing dog.

German dog owners cut their pudelhunds' hair. This made it easier for the dogs to swim. Now we call this a "poodle cut."

This is a dachshund puppy. Photo courtesy of Pixabay by Conger Design.

Poodles are just one of several breeds of dogs that were first bred in Germany. Others are Dachshunds, used to hunt badgers, Doberman Pinschers who were originally guard dogs, boxers for hunting and German Shepherds, who learned to be very good at herding sheep.

How well can dogs hear?

Have you ever heard someone blow a dog whistle and wondered why they seem to be blowing but there's no sound at all?

There is a sound, but you can't hear it. No human can.

The reason dogs can hear a dog whistle but people can't is that dogs' hearing range goes much higher than ours does. This is also true of some other animals, including cats and rodents, like mice and gerbils.

When you see your dog suddenly look up and look around as if he's hearing an interesting sound, that's true. He is.

He can also hear sounds like a police car siren before you can.

And if he howls when that police car, firetruck or ambulance passes your house, it's because for him the sound is loud and at a pitch that hurts his head. The howling helps him 'cover up' the painful sound until it goes away.

Too bad all dogs aren't like the Lundehund. They have the strange ability to close their ears when the world gets too loud!

Dogs have amazing noses.

Why do dogs always try to sniff everything?

Imagine that you're an animal that is born blind, deaf and unable to make any sound. You are totally helpless, except for just one thing.

You already have an incredibly good sense of smell. Because of this, you can find your mother and get some milk to grow strong.

If this was you, you'd be a newborn puppy.

Older puppies and adult dogs can see, hear and taste things, but for all their lives their sense of smell is their very first and best tool to get information about their world. It means everything to them!

As humans, we can only imagine how wonderful it would be to have a dog's fantastic ability to smell things.

Think about when you get home from school today. If you have a dog, they will be there at the door to greet you. But they aren't just there because they missed you! They want to know where you were.

Did you go somewhere fun?

Were there other people there, or other dogs?

Anyone they know?

And how were they today?

Did you have something nice to eat?

What was it?

And are you well?

Are you tired, or happy, or sad, or what?

Do you want to play?

Just a few sniffs and a dog can tell all these things! In fact, they can easily learn much more than we can in a conversation.

How do they do it?

It's all because of their super-noses. With it, they can tell all these things about another dog they meet:

How old are you?

Are you a boy or a girl?

If a girl, do you have puppies?

What did you eat today?

Where did you go? What did you do?

Are you happy?

Want to play?

Humans have about six million smell receptors in their noses. Smell receptors gather up a scent for the brain to analyze. Six million might sound like a lot. But dogs have 300 million smell receptors!

Humans take about 1 ½ second to sniff something. It takes that long to get the smell in your nose and then for your brain to know what it is.

Dogs can sniff as many as ten times every second! They do it while they are breathing in and while they are breathing out. Their nose and their brain is always sending them messages.

Dogs can smell layers of scents, not just one thing at a time. Since almost everything gives off an odour if you're a dog, that's a lot of information to take in. It is far more interesting than anything they see or hear.

Dogs can smell the trail of someone who just walked along a sidewalk or path a few minutes ago or as long as two days ago. They can follow this trail to know where that person or animal went.

Dogs always try to sniff everything because they get so much information this way. Many owners don't really like this, and try to teach their dogs to stop all this sniffing around and just keep walking.

When owners do this, dogs usually learn to look at their owner's face, body language and hand signals for information about why they're not stopping to get this wonderful information.

Dogs don't know that we can't smell nearly as well as they can.

This is an adult Dalmatian.

Can puppies' coats change colour?

Some can.

All Dalmatian puppies are born with pure white coats. They only get their spots as they get older.

Some mixed-breed puppies that are born grayish-black grow up to be black dogs.

But a dog's coat colour can also get lighter. A puppy that is black could have a silver coat as an adult. An orangey-gold puppy could become a cream-coloured adult.

Beagles have three colours as adults (these are black, white and orangey-brown) but they are born as two-coloured puppies (black and white).

Do dogs lose their baby teeth?

Yes, they do. Just like people.

Puppies are born with no teeth. Their 28 baby teeth soon grow in.

And, just like human babies, they want to bite everything with their new teeth.

But as they get a bit older, puppies lose their baby teeth, just like kids do. Their 42 adult teeth grow in.

Puppies always seem to be chewing things for the same reason babies do. It helps them know about their world. It also helps with the pain of their new teeth growing in.

To help puppies who are teething, give them a rubber chew toy that you put in the freezer for a few hours first. Be sure it is small enough that they can get their mouth around it. The coldness will help take away the teething pain.

This is a New Guinea Singing Dog. They sing to find their pack mates.

Can dogs sing?

The Singing Dog is a medium-sized wild dog that lives in New Guinea. Singing dogs look like they could be a pet dog. They have a reddish-gold or black-and-tan coat with some white markings. They live in the mountains and in forests and eat small reptiles, birds and small mammals. They are able to climb and jump just as well as a cat!

But the most unusual thing about Singing Dogs is their voice when they howl. It sounds very much like yodeling, something like a humpback whale's song.

When one Singing Dog starts to sing, others soon join in at different pitches, so you get a Singing Dog choir that is singing in harmony!

This is a search and rescue dog learning his new job for the United States Coast Guard.

You will likely never see Singing Dogs in the wild, but you can see them at some zoos. One place to see Singing Dogs and hear their strange songs is at the San Diego Zoo in California.

These Huskies work as a team. They can run for long distances in the coldest weather.

Dogs have an amazing ability to survive

Dogs are very good at surviving.

Surviving means staying alive, in times of trouble.

Just over a century ago, in 1912, the world's first super-sized ocean liner made its first and only trip across the Atlantic Ocean. It sailed from Ireland, where it was built and then to England to pick up passengers. Then it turned west, bound for New York City.

There were 2,223 people on board and 12 dogs. Most of them would never make it to New York.

This ship, called Titanic, was the biggest ship ever built, a wonder of the world at the time. The British owners of this ship, White Star Line, told everyone their new ship was the largest, grandest and safest boat ever built.

They said Titanic was unsinkable. That means that it was totally safe. It could never, ever sink.

But this boat had a terrible problem, even before it left Ireland. What almost no one knew was that there was a hidden fire on board, burning in one of the coal storage silos. (Titanic's power to run its three enormous propellers came from burning coal in its 162 furnaces).

After Titanic left England it never made it back to land.

Instead, this super ship hit an iceberg in the frigid ocean southeast of Newfoundland and east of Maine. This iceberg ripped a huge hole in the side of the ship because the steel used to make the ship's hull was weakened by the heat of the fire in the coal supply.

Slowly, the ship's hull filled with water. Two hours later, Titanic sank to the ocean's floor, where it remains today.

There weren't enough life-boats. Only 706 of the people survived, along with three of the dogs. All of them were rescued by crews of other ships and fishing boats from Newfoundland that went out into the stormy Atlantic to find them.

The dogs weren't in the lifeboats because there wasn't enough space for the people. No one really

This is a mixed breed.

knows how those three dogs could have survived in the frigid water. It is likely they found a piece of floating wreckage and were able to climb onto it. There they waited, hoping to be rescued.

Miraculously, they were.

Dogs are much better at surviving than humans in extremely cold places.

Sled dogs in the far North, including in Alaska, Northern Canada, Russia, Sweden, Finland, Greenland and Norway can sleep outside in any weather. They can survive in bitterly cold temperatures down to -76 degrees F. (-60 degrees C.)

This is Smokey, a Newfoundland dog.

Dogs with duck feet

All dogs can swim, but there are some breeds of dogs that have an extra swimming advantage. They have webbed feet.

One of these breeds is the Newfoundlander, or Newfie. They're a big dog with both webbed feet and a thick waterproof coat. They were bred by fishermen in Newfoundland to haul their nets, but soon showed that they are excellent at water rescue and lifesaving.

With a big, strong body, they are also known for their intelligence, loyalty and ability to stay calm in a crisis. These are all excellent abilities to have to help a person who is drowning.

Other breeds of dogs with webbed feet are the Portuguese Water Dog, German Wire-Haired Pointer, Nova Scotia Duck Tolling Retriever, Weimaraner, Chesapeake Bay Retriever, American Water Spaniel and Wirehaired Pointing Griffin.

Labrador Retrievers also have slightly webbed feet.

How smart are dogs?

Dogs have a brain that is as close to humans' brains as any animal's is. They are more like us and probably smarter than any other animal we keep as a pet, including cats.

Dogs rely on scent (what things smell like), instinct, memory and association (something they have learned) to do most their thinking. Some dogs are also very good at solving problems.

Just like children, young dogs learn very quickly when they have the opportunity to learn.

Wild dogs use all their intelligence to survive – that is, find water, food, shelter and a mate.

Dogs that live with people have many more opportunities to learn. Most dogs can learn about 150 words (cats can learn about 30 words). Some dogs learn far more words, as many as 1,000 words or more.

That's how many words one dog in England knows because his owner bought him 1,000 toys. He knows the name of every single one of his toys.

This only happened because his human took the time to teach him.

Dogs know how to look at people's faces and understand their expressions. This is something other animals (including pet cats) can't do.

Dogs can also read human body language, so they quickly learn to read hand signals. If you have ever seen videos of dancing dogs on YouTube, you might notice that the way the dog is able to know what steps or trick to do next is because their person is giving them signals. If you haven't, go have a look.

They're amazing!

Dogs are smart, especially when they have a kind and smart owner who takes them places and teaches them things like good manners, words and tricks!

Dogs started off as a wild animal that only knew how to do what all wild creatures know how to do, which is find water, food and shelter. But because dogs decided to move in with people, they have learned to do so many more things.

Living with people has changed dogs in many amazing ways.

And living with dogs has changed us, also in many amazing ways!

This Golden Retriever is having fun.

Thank you!

Thanks so much for reading this book. I really hope you enjoyed it learning about all these amazing fun facts about dogs!

Best wishes,

Jacquelyn

About Jacquelyn

Jacquelyn Elnor Johnson writes books about pets for children. Her family has just one pet, a cat named Boots. But in the past, there have been many wonderful dogs in her life, including Dachshunds, Poodles and a black Labrador Retriever.

She and her family live in Nova Scotia, Canada.

More fun pet and animal books you might like, all written for kids who are 9 to 12, or in grades three to seven:

Best Pets for Kids Series:

      I Want a Puppy, or a Dog

      I Want a Kitten, or a Cat

      I Want a Bearded Dragon

      I Want a Leopard Gecko

Fun Pets for Kids Series:

      Small Fun Pets; Beginner Pets for Kids 9-12

      Top 10 Fun Pets for Kids 9-12

Fun Animal Facts for Kids Series:

      Fun Dog Facts for Kids 9-12

      Fun Cat Facts for Kids 9-12

      Fun Leopard Gecko and Bearded Dragon Facts for Kids 9-12

      Fun Reptile Facts for Kids 9-12; Lizards, Turtles, Crocodilians, Snakes and Birds

Investigate more books for curious kids right here:

www.BestPetsForKids.fun

Made in the USA
Middletown, DE
19 December 2020